Table of Contents

- Chapter 1: Introduction to AI Model Optimization 2
  - The Importance of Model Optimization in AI 2
  - Overview of Model Optimization Techniques 3
  - Challenges in Optimizing AI Models 4
- Chapter 2: Low-Rank Adaptation (LoRA) for Model Optimization 5
  - Understanding Low-Rank Adaptation 5
  - Benefits of LoRA in Model Optimization 7
  - Implementation of LoRA in AI Models 8
- Chapter 3: Quantization Techniques for Model Optimization 9
  - Introduction to Quantization 9
  - Quantization Methods for Model Size Reduction 10
  - Case Studies on Quantization in AI Models 11
- Chapter 4: Compression Algorithms for Efficient Model Storage 13
  - Importance of Compression Algorithms in Model Optimization 13
  - Popular Compression Algorithms for AI Models 14
  - Implementing Compression Algorithms in AI Models 15
- Chapter 5: Model Optimization for Mobile and IoT Devices 16
  - Adapting AI Models for Mobile Devices 17
  - Optimizing AI Models for IoT Devices 17
  - Case Studies on Model Optimization for Mobile and IoT Devices 19
- Chapter 6: Resource-Efficient AI Models for Specific Applications 20
  - Optimizing AI Models for Healthcare Applications 20
  - Efficient AI Models for Autonomous Vehicles 21
  - Scalable AI Models for Small Businesses 22
- Chapter 7: Real-Time AI Model Optimization Techniques 24
  - Techniques for Reducing Inference Latency in AI Models 24
  - Implementing Real-Time Optimization in AI Models 25
  - Case Studies on Real-Time AI Model Optimization 26
- Chapter 8: Conclusion and Future Trends in AI Model Optimization 27

Summary of Techniques for Professionals 27
Emerging Trends in AI Model Optimization 28
Recommendations for Professionals in Model Optimization 29

Chapter 1: Introduction to AI Model Optimization

The Importance of Model Optimization in AI

Model optimization is a crucial aspect of AI development, especially in today's landscape where the costs and availability of GPUs are becoming increasingly challenging. With the rising demand for AI capabilities, there is a need to make models smaller and more efficient to reduce the dependency on large-scale infrastructure. Techniques like Low-Rank Adaptation (LoRA) and Quantization are playing a significant role in achieving this goal, allowing smaller players and startups to access sophisticated AI capabilities without breaking the bank.

One of the key benefits of model optimization is the development of low-power AI models for edge computing. These models are designed to run efficiently on devices with limited computational resources, making them ideal for applications where real-time processing is essential. By optimizing AI models for edge computing, developers can ensure that their solutions are accessible and usable in a wide range of scenarios, from smart homes to industrial automation.

Quantization techniques are another important tool in the model optimization toolbox, as they help reduce the size of AI models without sacrificing performance. By quantizing the parameters of a model, developers can significantly reduce the amount of memory required to store and run the model, making it more accessible for deployment on a variety of devices. This is particularly important for applications where storage and memory constraints are a concern, such as mobile devices and IoT devices.

Compression algorithms are also a key component of model optimization, as they enable efficient storage and transfer of AI models. By compressing the parameters of a model, developers can reduce the overall size of the model without compromising its performance, making it easier to deploy and manage in a variety of environments. This is particularly important for applications where bandwidth and storage space are limited, such as in healthcare applications and autonomous vehicles.

Overall, model optimization plays a crucial role in making AI more accessible and efficient for a wide range of applications. By leveraging techniques like Low-Rank Adaptation, Quantization, and Compression, developers can create resource-efficient AI models that are suitable for deployment on a variety of devices and platforms. Whether it's for edge computing, mobile devices, IoT devices, or real-time applications, optimizing AI models is essential for ensuring that AI technology remains accessible and usable for all.

Overview of Model Optimization Techniques

The subchapter "Overview of Model Optimization Techniques" delves into the various methods and strategies that professionals can employ to optimize AI models. With the rising costs and scarcity of GPUs, there is a growing need for AI models to be smaller and more efficient. Techniques such as Low-Rank Adaptation (LoRA) and Quantization are playing a crucial role in making sophisticated AI capabilities accessible to smaller players and startups. By reducing the dependency on large-scale infrastructure, these techniques are enabling organizations to develop and deploy AI models more efficiently.

One key aspect of model optimization is the development of low-power AI models for edge computing. Edge devices have limited computational resources and energy constraints, making it imperative to design models that are both accurate and resource-efficient. Quantization techniques, which involve reducing the precision of numerical values, are particularly useful in reducing the size of AI models without significantly compromising performance. This allows for more efficient model storage and deployment on edge devices, enabling real-time processing of data without the need for constant connectivity to the cloud.

In addition to edge computing, model optimization is also crucial for mobile and IoT devices. With the proliferation of smartphones, wearables, and connected devices, there is a growing need for resource-efficient AI models that can run on these devices without draining battery life. Techniques such as compression algorithms and model optimization specifically tailored for mobile and IoT applications are essential in ensuring that AI capabilities can be seamlessly integrated into these devices.

Furthermore, model optimization techniques are also vital for specific industry applications, such as healthcare and autonomous vehicles. In healthcare, resource-efficient AI models can help improve diagnosis accuracy and treatment outcomes, while in autonomous vehicles, scalable AI models are essential for real-time decision-making and navigation. By optimizing AI models for these specialized applications, professionals can ensure that AI capabilities are effectively integrated into various industries, improving efficiency and performance.

Overall, the subchapter "Overview of Model Optimization Techniques" highlights the importance of optimizing AI models for various applications and industries. By employing techniques such as quantization, compression, and low-power design, professionals can develop AI models that are not only efficient but also accessible to a wider range of users. Whether for edge computing, mobile devices, or industry-specific applications, model optimization is essential for unlocking the full potential of AI technologies in today's rapidly evolving digital landscape.

Challenges in Optimizing AI Models

Optimizing AI models has become increasingly important in today's fast-paced technological landscape. With the rising costs and scarcity of GPUs, there is a growing need to make AI models smaller and more efficient. However, this process comes with its own set of challenges that professionals in the field must navigate.

One of the main challenges in optimizing AI models is ensuring that the model remains accurate and reliable after optimization. Techniques like Low-Rank Adaptation (LoRA) and Quantization can help reduce the size of AI models, but if not implemented carefully, they can also lead to a loss of accuracy. Professionals must strike a balance between model size and performance to ensure that the optimized model still meets the desired outcomes.

Another challenge in optimizing AI models is ensuring that the model is accessible to smaller players and startups. While large-scale infrastructure can support the training and deployment of complex AI models, smaller organizations may not have the resources to do so. Techniques like low-power AI models for edge computing and compression algorithms for efficient model storage can help make sophisticated AI capabilities accessible to a wider audience.

Additionally, optimizing AI models for specific use cases, such as mobile devices, IoT devices, healthcare applications, and autonomous vehicles, poses its own set of challenges. Each of these applications has unique requirements and constraints that must be taken into account during the optimization process. Professionals must consider factors like resource efficiency, inference latency, and scalability when optimizing AI models for these specialized use cases.

In conclusion, while there are many benefits to optimizing AI models, there are also several challenges that professionals must overcome. By carefully balancing model size and performance, making AI capabilities accessible to smaller players, and considering the unique requirements of specific use cases, professionals can successfully optimize AI models for a variety of applications. By staying informed on the latest techniques and best practices in model optimization, professionals can navigate these challenges and unlock the full potential of AI technology.

Chapter 2: Low-Rank Adaptation (LoRA) for Model Optimization

Understanding Low-Rank Adaptation

In the world of artificial intelligence, there is a growing need for optimizing AI models to be smaller and more efficient. With the rising costs and scarcity of GPUs, there is a push towards making sophisticated AI capabilities accessible to smaller players and startups. One technique that is helping to achieve this goal is Low-Rank Adaptation (LoRA). LoRA is a method that involves reducing the rank of the weight matrices in a neural network, which can significantly decrease the computational complexity of the model without sacrificing accuracy.

Another key technique for optimizing AI models is Quantization. This method involves reducing the precision of the weights and activations in a neural network, which can lead to a significant reduction in model size. By quantizing the parameters of a neural network, it is possible to achieve a smaller memory footprint and faster inference times, making it ideal for edge computing and resource-constrained environments.

Compression algorithms are also essential for efficient model storage. These algorithms enable the reduction of the size of AI models without compromising their performance. By applying compression techniques, such as pruning or weight sharing, it is possible to create more compact models that are easier to deploy and manage, particularly in scenarios where storage space is limited.

Optimizing AI models for mobile devices is another critical area of focus. By designing models that are specifically tailored for smartphones and tablets, developers can ensure that their applications run smoothly and efficiently on these devices. Techniques such as model quantization and compression can be particularly valuable in this context, as they can help reduce the computational burden on mobile processors while maintaining high levels of accuracy.

Overall, understanding low-rank adaptation and other optimization techniques is essential for professionals working in the field of model optimization and accessibility. By implementing these strategies, developers can create AI models that are smaller, more efficient, and better suited for a wide range of applications, from healthcare and autonomous vehicles to IoT devices and real-time applications. Ultimately, the goal is to make AI more accessible and scalable for all businesses, regardless of size or resources.

Benefits of LoRA in Model Optimization

In the world of AI model optimization, one technique that is gaining traction is Low-Rank Adaptation (LoRA). LoRA is particularly beneficial for professionals in the field of model optimization and accessibility. With the rising costs and scarcity of GPUs, there is a push towards optimizing AI models to be smaller and more efficient. LoRA is helping to make sophisticated AI capabilities accessible to smaller players and startups, reducing the dependency on large-scale infrastructure. This means that even those with limited resources can now optimize their AI models without breaking the bank.

One of the key benefits of LoRA is its ability to create low-power AI models for edge computing. Edge computing is becoming increasingly popular as it allows for data processing to be done closer to the source, reducing latency and improving efficiency. By using LoRA, professionals can create AI models that are optimized for edge computing, making them ideal for a wide range of applications.

In addition to low-power AI models, LoRA also enables professionals to utilize quantization techniques for reducing model size. Quantization is a process that involves reducing the precision of weights and activations in a neural network, which in turn reduces the size of the model. This not only makes the model more efficient but also reduces the amount of memory required to store it. By combining LoRA with quantization techniques, professionals can create AI models that are not only smaller but also more resource-efficient.

Furthermore, LoRA allows for the use of compression algorithms for efficient model storage. This is particularly important for professionals who work with large datasets and need to store multiple AI models. By using LoRA, they can compress their models in a way that reduces storage requirements without compromising on performance. This means that professionals can optimize their AI models without having to worry about running out of storage space.

Overall, the benefits of LoRA in model optimization are vast and varied. From creating low-power AI models for edge computing to reducing model size through quantization techniques, LoRA is helping professionals in the field of model optimization and accessibility to streamline their processes and make their AI models more efficient. With the help of LoRA, professionals can create resource-efficient AI models for a wide range of applications, from healthcare to autonomous vehicles, and beyond.

Implementation of LoRA in AI Models

In the subchapter titled "Implementation of LoRA in AI Models," we will explore how Low-Rank Adaptation (LoRA) is revolutionizing the field of model optimization and accessibility for professionals. With the rising costs and scarcity of GPUs, there is a growing need to optimize AI models to be smaller and more efficient. LoRA, along with other techniques such as Quantization, is playing a crucial role in making sophisticated AI capabilities more accessible to smaller players and startups, reducing the dependency on large-scale infrastructure.

One of the key benefits of implementing LoRA in AI models is the development of low-power models for edge computing. By leveraging the power of LoRA, professionals can create AI models that are optimized for running on devices with limited computational resources, making them ideal for edge computing applications where real-time processing is essential. This not only reduces the energy consumption of AI models but also improves their efficiency and performance.

Furthermore, Quantization techniques can be used in conjunction with LoRA to reduce the size of AI models without compromising their accuracy. By quantizing the weights and activations of neural networks, professionals can significantly decrease the storage requirements of models, making them more suitable for deployment on resource-constrained devices such as mobile phones and IoT devices. This enables the development of efficient AI models that can be easily deployed in a wide range of applications, from healthcare to autonomous vehicles.

In addition to reducing model size, compression algorithms can also be applied to optimize AI models for efficient storage and deployment. By compressing the parameters of neural networks, professionals can create models that take up less memory and have faster inference times, making them ideal for real-time applications where speed is of the essence. This opens up new possibilities for the development of resource-efficient AI models that can be deployed in a variety of industries, from healthcare to small businesses.

Overall, the implementation of LoRA in AI models is playing a pivotal role in advancing the field of model optimization and accessibility for professionals. By leveraging techniques such as Quantization, compression algorithms, and model optimization, professionals can create efficient, scalable, and resource-efficient AI models that are suitable for a wide range of applications, from edge computing to real-time processing. With the right tools and techniques, professionals can unlock the full potential of AI technology and drive innovation in their respective industries.

Chapter 3: Quantization Techniques for Model Optimization

Introduction to Quantization

In the dynamic world of artificial intelligence, the need for optimizing AI models has become more apparent than ever. With the rising costs and scarcity of GPUs, there is a push towards making AI models smaller and more efficient. This push has led to the development of techniques like Low-Rank Adaptation (LoRA) and Quantization, which are helping to make sophisticated AI capabilities accessible to smaller players and startups. By reducing the dependency on large-scale infrastructure, these techniques are revolutionizing the way AI models are developed and deployed.

Quantization, in particular, is a powerful technique that is gaining momentum in the field of model optimization and accessibility. By reducing the precision of numerical values in a model, quantization can significantly shrink the size of the model without compromising its performance. This allows for the creation of low-power AI models that are ideal for edge computing, where resources are limited. By implementing quantization techniques, developers can create efficient AI models that can be deployed on mobile devices, IoT devices, healthcare applications, autonomous vehicles, and more.

Compression algorithms are another key aspect of model optimization that is crucial for efficient model storage. By compressing the parameters of an AI model, developers can reduce the storage requirements of the model, making it easier to deploy and manage on various platforms. This is particularly important for small businesses and startups that may not have access to large-scale infrastructure but still want to leverage the power of AI in their applications.

In this subchapter, we will explore the various quantization techniques, compression algorithms, and model optimization strategies that are essential for creating resource-efficient AI models. We will delve into the challenges and opportunities involved in optimizing AI models for different applications, from real-time applications to edge computing. By understanding these techniques and strategies, professionals in the field of model optimization can stay ahead of the curve and deliver cutting-edge AI solutions that are accessible to all.

Quantization Methods for Model Size Reduction

Quantization methods for model size reduction are becoming increasingly popular as the need for smaller and more efficient AI models grows. With the rising costs and scarcity of GPUs, there is a push towards optimizing AI models to be more accessible to smaller players and startups. Techniques like Low-Rank Adaptation (LoRA) and Quantization are helping to make sophisticated AI capabilities available to a wider audience, reducing the dependency on large-scale infrastructure.

One of the key benefits of quantization techniques is the reduction in model size. By representing weights and activations with fewer bits, the overall size of the model can be significantly reduced without compromising performance. This is particularly important for low-power AI models used in edge computing, where resources are limited and efficiency is crucial.

Compression algorithms are also being used to efficiently store AI models. By removing redundancy and unnecessary information, compression techniques can further reduce the size of the model without sacrificing accuracy. This is important for applications where storage space is limited, such as mobile devices or IoT devices.

In addition to reducing model size, optimization techniques are also being used to improve the efficiency of AI models for specific applications. For example, resource-efficient AI models are being developed for healthcare applications, where speed and accuracy are critical. Similarly, efficient AI models are being designed for autonomous vehicles, where real-time decision-making is essential.

Overall, quantization methods are playing a crucial role in making AI models more accessible and efficient for a wide range of applications. By reducing model size, improving storage efficiency, and optimizing for specific use cases, professionals are able to develop scalable and resource-efficient AI models that can meet the needs of small businesses, real-time applications, and a variety of other niches.

Case Studies on Quantization in AI Models

Quantization is a technique that has gained popularity in the field of AI model optimization. This technique involves reducing the precision of the weights and activations in a neural network, which in turn decreases the memory footprint and computational complexity of the model. By quantizing a model, it becomes more efficient and suitable for deployment on low-power devices such as smartphones, IoT devices, and edge computing systems. In this subchapter, we will explore some case studies that demonstrate the effectiveness of quantization in improving the accessibility and efficiency of AI models.

One case study focuses on the development of low-power AI models for edge computing. By applying quantization techniques to reduce the model size, researchers were able to deploy sophisticated AI capabilities on resource-constrained edge devices without compromising performance. This has opened up new possibilities for real-time processing of data at the edge, enabling applications such as smart surveillance, predictive maintenance, and autonomous systems.

Another case study showcases the use of quantization techniques to optimize AI models for mobile devices. By compressing the model using quantization algorithms, developers were able to create lightweight and efficient models that could run smoothly on smartphones and tablets. This not only improves the user experience by reducing latency and improving battery life but also makes AI-powered applications more accessible to a wider audience.

In the healthcare industry, quantization has been instrumental in developing resource-efficient AI models for various applications. By reducing the size of the models, researchers were able to deploy AI algorithms on medical devices and equipment, allowing for real-time analysis of patient data and improving diagnostic accuracy. This has the potential to revolutionize healthcare delivery by enabling faster and more accurate diagnoses, particularly in remote or underserved areas.

In the realm of autonomous vehicles, quantization techniques have been used to create efficient AI models that can process sensor data in real-time. By optimizing the models for reduced inference latency, researchers were able to enhance the safety and performance of autonomous systems, making them more reliable and responsive to changing road conditions. This has significant implications for the future of transportation, as AI-powered vehicles become increasingly prevalent on our roads.

Overall, these case studies illustrate the power of quantization in making AI models more accessible, efficient, and scalable across a variety of industries and applications. By leveraging techniques like quantization, professionals can optimize their AI models for deployment on a wide range of devices and platforms, paving the way for a more decentralized and democratized AI ecosystem.

Chapter 4: Compression Algorithms for Efficient Model Storage

Importance of Compression Algorithms in Model Optimization

In the rapidly evolving field of AI, the importance of compression algorithms in model optimization cannot be overstated. With the rising costs and scarcity of GPUs, there is a growing need to optimize AI models to be smaller and more efficient. This is where techniques like Low-Rank Adaptation (LoRA) and Quantization come into play, helping to make sophisticated AI capabilities more accessible to smaller players and startups. By reducing the dependency on large-scale infrastructure, these techniques are enabling a wider range of individuals and organizations to leverage the power of AI.

One of the key benefits of compression algorithms in model optimization is the ability to create low-power AI models for edge computing. These models are designed to operate efficiently on devices with limited computational resources, making them ideal for applications where real-time processing is crucial. By reducing the size of AI models through quantization techniques, developers can ensure that their models are not only compact but also resource-efficient, making them well-suited for deployment in a variety of environments.

Another important aspect of compression algorithms in model optimization is efficient model storage. By compressing AI models, developers can reduce the amount of storage space required to store these models, making them easier to manage and deploy. This is particularly important for mobile devices, IoT devices, and other applications where storage space is limited. By optimizing AI models for these platforms, developers can ensure that their models are both efficient and effective in a wide range of scenarios.

In addition to improving storage efficiency, compression algorithms can also help to reduce inference latency in AI models. By compressing models and optimizing them for real-time applications, developers can ensure that their models are able to provide rapid responses to user inputs. This is crucial for applications such as autonomous vehicles, healthcare, and other time-sensitive scenarios where speed is of the essence.

Overall, the importance of compression algorithms in model optimization cannot be understated. By leveraging techniques like Low-Rank Adaptation, Quantization, and other compression algorithms, developers can create AI models that are smaller, more efficient, and better suited for a wide range of applications. Whether it's for edge computing, mobile devices, IoT devices, or real-time applications, compression algorithms are essential tools for optimizing AI models in today's fast-paced world.

Popular Compression Algorithms for AI Models

In the ever-evolving world of artificial intelligence, the need for optimization and efficiency is more crucial than ever. With the rising costs and scarcity of GPUs, there is a growing push towards making AI models smaller and more efficient. This has led to the development and popularity of various compression algorithms that help reduce model size without compromising on performance.

One popular technique that has gained traction in recent years is Low-Rank Adaptation (LoRA). LoRA is a method that leverages the low-rank structure of neural networks to reduce the number of parameters and computations required for inference. By exploiting the inherent redundancy in neural network weights, LoRA can significantly compress model size while maintaining accuracy.

Another widely used technique for model compression is quantization. Quantization involves reducing the precision of weights and activations in a neural network, thereby reducing the memory footprint of the model. By quantizing weights and activations to lower bit-widths, such as 8-bit or even binary values, practitioners can achieve substantial reductions in model size with minimal loss in performance.

Compression algorithms are also essential for efficient model storage and deployment. These algorithms help optimize the storage and transfer of AI models, making them more accessible and scalable for a variety of applications. By compressing models using techniques like pruning, weight sharing, and Huffman coding, practitioners can reduce the memory and processing requirements of AI models, making them more suitable for deployment on resource-constrained devices.

In the realm of edge computing, where low-power AI models are essential for real-time applications, compression algorithms play a crucial role in enabling efficient inference on devices with limited computational resources. By optimizing AI models for mobile and IoT devices, practitioners can bring sophisticated AI capabilities to a broader range of applications, from healthcare to autonomous vehicles, without compromising on performance or accuracy.

In conclusion, the popularity of compression algorithms for AI models is on the rise, driven by the need for smaller, more efficient models that can be deployed on a wide range of devices.

Techniques like Low-Rank Adaptation, quantization, and other compression algorithms are helping make sophisticated AI capabilities more accessible and scalable for a variety of industries and applications. By optimizing AI models for resource-efficient deployment, practitioners can unlock the full potential of artificial intelligence in a wide range of real-time and edge computing applications.

Implementing Compression Algorithms in AI Models

Implementing compression algorithms in AI models is a crucial aspect of optimizing AI models for professionals in the field. With the rising costs and scarcity of GPUs, there is a growing need to make AI models smaller and more efficient. Techniques like Low-Rank Adaptation (LoRA) and Quantization are playing a key role in achieving this goal. These techniques are making sophisticated AI capabilities accessible to smaller players and startups, reducing the dependency on large-scale infrastructure.

One of the key benefits of implementing compression algorithms in AI models is the ability to create low-power AI models for edge computing. Edge computing is becoming increasingly popular as it allows for data processing to happen closer to the source, reducing latency and improving efficiency. By compressing AI models, professionals can create models that are suitable for edge computing applications without compromising on performance.

Quantization techniques are another important aspect of implementing compression algorithms in AI models. These techniques involve reducing the precision of the model weights and activations, resulting in a smaller model size. This is especially useful for professionals looking to reduce the memory footprint of their AI models, making them more efficient and accessible for a wider range of applications.

Compression algorithms also play a crucial role in efficient model storage. By compressing AI models, professionals can reduce the amount of storage space required, making it easier to deploy and manage models in various environments. This is particularly important for mobile devices, IoT devices, healthcare applications, autonomous vehicles, and small businesses where storage space may be limited.

In conclusion, implementing compression algorithms in AI models is essential for professionals looking to optimize their models for various applications. By utilizing techniques like Low-Rank Adaptation, Quantization, and other compression algorithms, professionals can create resource-efficient AI models that are suitable for a wide range of use cases. Whether it's reducing model size, improving inference latency, or optimizing for real-time applications, compression algorithms are a powerful tool for achieving model optimization and accessibility in the field of AI.

Chapter 5: Model Optimization for Mobile and IoT Devices

Adapting AI Models for Mobile Devices

In the world of AI model optimization, one of the key challenges faced by professionals is adapting these models for mobile devices. With the increasing popularity of smartphones and tablets, there is a growing demand for AI capabilities to be accessible on these devices. However, the limited processing power and memory of mobile devices present a unique set of challenges when it comes to running complex AI models.

To address these challenges, techniques like Low-Rank Adaptation (LoRA) and Quantization are being employed to make AI models smaller and more efficient. LoRA helps in reducing the computational complexity of AI models, making them more suitable for mobile devices with limited resources. Quantization, on the other hand, reduces the precision of model parameters, leading to smaller model sizes and faster inference times on mobile devices.

Moreover, the development of low-power AI models for edge computing has further revolutionized the field of AI model optimization for mobile devices. These models are designed to run efficiently on devices with low power consumption, making them ideal for applications in remote locations or areas with limited access to electricity.

In addition, compression algorithms are being used to efficiently store AI models on mobile devices, further reducing the memory footprint and allowing for faster model loading times. This is crucial for real-time applications where speed and efficiency are of utmost importance.

Overall, the optimization of AI models for mobile devices is essential for making sophisticated AI capabilities accessible to a wider audience. By employing techniques like LoRA, Quantization, and compression algorithms, professionals can ensure that AI models run smoothly and efficiently on mobile devices, opening up new possibilities for AI applications in various industries.

Optimizing AI Models for IoT Devices

Optimizing AI models for IoT devices is crucial in order to ensure that these devices can effectively process data and make decisions in real-time. With the increasing prevalence of IoT devices in various industries, the need for efficient and resource-friendly AI models has never been greater. Techniques like Low-Rank Adaptation (LoRA) and Quantization are playing a key role in making AI models more accessible and practical for IoT applications.

Low-power AI models for edge computing are essential for IoT devices that operate on limited battery power or have limited processing capabilities. These models are designed to be lightweight and efficient, allowing them to run on resource-constrained devices without compromising performance. By optimizing AI models for edge computing, developers can ensure that IoT devices can process data locally and make decisions quickly without relying on cloud-based services.

Quantization techniques are also important for reducing the size of AI models, making them more suitable for deployment on IoT devices. By quantizing the parameters of a model, developers can reduce the memory and computational requirements, allowing the model to run efficiently on devices with limited resources. This not only improves the performance of the AI model but also reduces the cost and energy consumption associated with running complex models on IoT devices.

Compression algorithms play a crucial role in optimizing AI models for IoT devices by reducing the storage requirements without compromising the accuracy of the model. By using compression techniques, developers can ensure that AI models can be deployed on devices with limited storage capacity, making them more accessible and practical for a wide range of applications. This is particularly important for IoT devices that need to operate in remote or resource-constrained environments where storage space is limited.

In conclusion, optimizing AI models for IoT devices is essential for ensuring that these devices can operate efficiently and effectively in a wide range of applications. By using techniques like Low-Rank Adaptation, Quantization, and compression algorithms, developers can create AI models that are lightweight, efficient, and practical for deployment on IoT devices. This not only improves the performance of IoT devices but also reduces the cost and energy consumption associated with running complex AI models, making them more accessible to a wider range of industries and applications.

Case Studies on Model Optimization for Mobile and IoT Devices

In this subchapter, we will explore various case studies on model optimization for mobile and IoT devices. With the increasing demand for AI capabilities on smaller and more efficient devices, it has become crucial to optimize models to ensure optimal performance while conserving resources. Techniques like Low-Rank Adaptation (LoRA) and Quantization have emerged as game-changers in this space, enabling even startups and small players to leverage sophisticated AI capabilities without the need for large-scale infrastructure.

One case study that exemplifies the power of model optimization for mobile devices is the development of low-power AI models for edge computing. By optimizing models to run efficiently on mobile devices, companies can leverage AI capabilities at the edge without draining battery life or requiring constant connectivity to the cloud. This has significant implications for industries like healthcare and autonomous vehicles, where real-time processing is essential.

Another case study showcases the use of quantization techniques for reducing model size on IoT devices. By quantizing the weights of neural networks, companies can drastically reduce the memory footprint of their models without sacrificing accuracy. This is particularly important in IoT applications where resources are limited, and efficiency is paramount. Compression algorithms further enhance this optimization by enabling efficient model storage on devices with constrained storage capacity.

Furthermore, model optimization for mobile and IoT devices is essential for real-time applications where reducing inference latency is critical. By optimizing models to run efficiently on resource-constrained devices, companies can ensure real-time processing of data without compromising accuracy. This is especially important in industries like healthcare, where timely insights can have life-saving implications.

Overall, these case studies underscore the importance of model optimization for mobile and IoT devices in making AI capabilities accessible to a wide range of industries and applications. By leveraging techniques like LoRA, quantization, and compression, companies can develop resource-efficient AI models that meet the demands of today's fast-paced, data-driven world.

Chapter 6: Resource-Efficient AI Models for Specific Applications

Optimizing AI Models for Healthcare Applications

Optimizing AI models for healthcare applications is crucial in ensuring that medical professionals have access to accurate and efficient tools to improve patient outcomes. With the rising costs and scarcity of GPUs, there is a push towards optimizing AI models to be smaller and more efficient. Techniques like Low-Rank Adaptation (LoRA) and Quantization are helping make sophisticated AI capabilities accessible to smaller players and startups, reducing the dependency on large-scale infrastructure. By implementing these techniques, healthcare organizations can benefit from cost-effective AI solutions that can deliver high-quality results.

One key aspect of optimizing AI models for healthcare applications is developing low-power AI models for edge computing. Edge computing allows AI models to run on local devices, reducing the need for constant connectivity to cloud servers. This not only improves the speed of data processing but also enhances data privacy and security. By optimizing AI models for edge computing, healthcare professionals can access real-time insights and make timely decisions without relying on external servers.

Quantization techniques play a crucial role in reducing the size of AI models, making them more efficient and accessible for healthcare applications. By quantizing model parameters, researchers can minimize memory usage and computational resources without compromising on model accuracy. This is particularly important in healthcare settings where data storage and processing constraints can limit the adoption of AI technologies. By implementing quantization techniques, healthcare organizations can deploy AI models on a wider range of devices and platforms, improving accessibility and scalability.

Compression algorithms are another valuable tool in optimizing AI models for healthcare applications. These algorithms reduce the size of model files, making them easier to store and deploy on various devices. By compressing AI models, healthcare professionals can efficiently manage their resources and ensure that critical medical data is accessible whenever and wherever it is needed. This optimization technique is especially beneficial for mobile devices and IoT devices, where storage space and processing power are limited.

In conclusion, optimizing AI models for healthcare applications is essential for improving patient care and driving innovation in the medical field. By implementing techniques like Low-Rank Adaptation, Quantization, and Compression algorithms, healthcare organizations can develop resource-efficient AI models that are accessible, scalable, and efficient. With the right optimization strategies in place, medical professionals can leverage AI technologies to provide better diagnosis, treatment, and personalized care to patients, ultimately transforming the healthcare industry for the better.

Efficient AI Models for Autonomous Vehicles

Efficient AI models for autonomous vehicles have become a key focus in the field of artificial intelligence. As the demand for autonomous vehicles continues to grow, there is a need for AI models that are not only accurate but also efficient in terms of computation and storage. This subchapter will explore some of the latest techniques and strategies being used to optimize AI models for autonomous vehicles, ensuring they are able to operate with maximum efficiency.

One of the main challenges in developing AI models for autonomous vehicles is the need for real-time decision making. This requires models that are not only accurate but also able to process data quickly and efficiently. Techniques such as Low-Rank Adaptation (LoRA) and Quantization are being used to reduce the size and complexity of AI models, making them more suitable for the limited computational resources available in autonomous vehicles.

Another key consideration in developing efficient AI models for autonomous vehicles is the need for low-power consumption. Edge computing has become increasingly important in this context, as it allows for data processing to be performed closer to the source, reducing the need for large amounts of computational power. By developing low-power AI models that can operate efficiently on edge devices, researchers are able to ensure that autonomous vehicles can operate for longer periods of time without needing to recharge.

In addition to reducing the size and power consumption of AI models for autonomous vehicles, researchers are also exploring compression algorithms for efficient model storage. By compressing AI models without sacrificing accuracy, developers are able to ensure that autonomous vehicles have access to the data they need without requiring large amounts of storage space.

Overall, the optimization of AI models for autonomous vehicles is a complex and challenging task. By leveraging techniques such as Low-Rank Adaptation, Quantization, edge computing, and compression algorithms, researchers are able to develop efficient AI models that are capable of making real-time decisions while operating with minimal power consumption and storage requirements. These advancements are helping to pave the way for a future where autonomous vehicles are not only safe and reliable but also able to operate with maximum efficiency.

Scalable AI Models for Small Businesses

In today's ever-evolving technological landscape, small businesses are increasingly recognizing the importance of incorporating AI models into their operations to stay competitive. However, the high costs and limited availability of GPUs often present significant barriers to entry for smaller players. As a result, there is a growing demand for scalable AI models that are both efficient and accessible. Techniques like Low-Rank Adaptation (LoRA) and Quantization are revolutionizing the field by enabling sophisticated AI capabilities in a more compact and cost-effective manner.

One key area of focus in the development of scalable AI models is edge computing. Low-power AI models designed for edge devices are becoming increasingly popular due to their ability to process data locally, reducing dependence on cloud infrastructure and minimizing latency. By optimizing AI models for edge computing, small businesses can achieve faster and more efficient decision-making processes, ultimately leading to improved operational efficiency and cost savings.

Quantization techniques are another powerful tool in the arsenal of AI model optimization. By reducing the precision of model weights and activations, quantization can dramatically decrease the size of AI models without compromising performance. This is particularly beneficial for small businesses with limited resources, as it allows them to deploy AI models on devices with constrained storage and computational capabilities.

In addition to quantization, compression algorithms play a crucial role in optimizing AI models for small businesses. These algorithms help to efficiently store and transmit model parameters, reducing the overall footprint of the model without sacrificing accuracy or performance. By implementing compression techniques, small businesses can leverage AI capabilities without breaking the bank on expensive hardware or infrastructure.

Overall, the development of scalable AI models is a game-changer for small businesses looking to harness the power of artificial intelligence. By leveraging techniques like Low-Rank Adaptation, Quantization, and compression algorithms, smaller players can access sophisticated AI capabilities that were once reserved for larger organizations. As the demand for AI continues to grow across industries, the ability to optimize and scale AI models will be essential for small businesses to stay competitive in an increasingly digital world.

Chapter 7: Real-Time AI Model Optimization Techniques

Techniques for Reducing Inference Latency in AI Models

In the fast-paced world of artificial intelligence, reducing inference latency in AI models is crucial for ensuring optimal performance and efficiency. Techniques such as Low-Rank Adaptation (LoRA) and Quantization are revolutionizing the way AI models are optimized, making sophisticated capabilities accessible to smaller players and startups. By reducing the dependency on large-scale infrastructure, these techniques are helping to level the playing field and empower a wider range of professionals to harness the power of AI.

One of the key benefits of techniques like LoRA and Quantization is their ability to create low-power AI models that are ideal for edge computing. This allows for real-time processing of data directly on devices, without the need for constant communication with a central server. By optimizing AI models for edge computing, professionals can significantly reduce latency and improve overall performance, making AI more accessible and efficient for a variety of applications.

Quantization techniques are also playing a vital role in reducing model size, making it easier to store and deploy AI models efficiently. By converting floating-point numbers to fixed-point numbers, professionals can drastically reduce the memory and computational resources required for inference, leading to faster processing times and lower latency. This is especially important for mobile devices and IoT devices, where limited resources can pose a challenge for running complex AI models.

Compression algorithms are another valuable tool for optimizing AI models and reducing latency. By removing redundant information and minimizing the size of the model, compression algorithms make it easier to store and deploy AI models in resource-constrained environments. This is particularly beneficial for applications in healthcare, autonomous vehicles, and small businesses, where efficient use of resources is essential for success.

In conclusion, techniques for reducing inference latency in AI models are essential for optimizing performance and efficiency in a wide range of applications. By embracing techniques like LoRA, Quantization, compression algorithms, and model optimization, professionals can create resource-efficient AI models that are accessible and scalable for various industries. With the right tools and strategies, professionals can unlock the full potential of AI and drive innovation in real-time applications, edge computing, and more.

Implementing Real-Time Optimization in AI Models

Implementing real-time optimization in AI models is crucial for ensuring that these models can perform efficiently in various applications. With the rising costs and scarcity of GPUs, there is a growing need to optimize AI models to be smaller and more efficient. This push towards optimization has led to the development of techniques like Low-Rank Adaptation (LoRA) and Quantization, which are making sophisticated AI capabilities accessible to smaller players and startups.

One of the key benefits of implementing real-time optimization in AI models is the ability to create low-power AI models for edge computing. These optimized models can run on devices with limited resources, making them ideal for applications where power consumption is a concern. Techniques like quantization can also help reduce the size of AI models, making them more efficient and easier to deploy on edge devices.

Another important aspect of real-time optimization in AI models is the development of compression algorithms for efficient model storage. By compressing AI models, developers can reduce the amount of storage space required, making it easier to deploy these models on a wide range of devices. This is particularly important for mobile devices, IoT devices, and other resource-constrained environments.

In addition to optimizing AI models for efficiency and storage, it is also important to consider their performance in real-time applications. Techniques for reducing inference latency in AI models are crucial for ensuring that these models can respond quickly to changing input data. This is especially important in applications where real-time decision-making is required, such as autonomous vehicles and healthcare applications.

Overall, implementing real-time optimization in AI models is essential for ensuring that these models can perform efficiently in a wide range of applications. By using techniques like low-rank adaptation, quantization, and compression algorithms, developers can create resource-efficient and scalable AI models that are accessible to a diverse range of users, from small businesses to large enterprises.

Case Studies on Real-Time AI Model Optimization

In the subchapter titled "Case Studies on Real-Time AI Model Optimization," we will delve into real-world examples of how professionals are implementing techniques to optimize AI models for real-time applications. These case studies will provide valuable insights into the challenges faced and the innovative solutions developed to overcome them.

One case study focuses on a startup in the healthcare industry that needed to optimize their AI model for real-time processing on edge devices. By implementing Quantization techniques and Compression algorithms, they were able to reduce the size of their model significantly without compromising on accuracy. This enabled them to deploy their AI solution on a wider range of devices, making it more accessible to healthcare providers in remote areas.

Another case study showcases a small business in the autonomous vehicle industry that needed to optimize their AI model for resource-efficient processing. By leveraging techniques like Low-Rank Adaptation (LoRA) and Scalable AI models, they were able to reduce the computational resources required for inference, making their autonomous vehicles more cost-effective and scalable.

Furthermore, a case study on AI model optimization for IoT devices highlights the importance of developing low-power AI models that can run efficiently on battery-operated devices. By utilizing techniques for reducing inference latency and optimizing for mobile devices, companies in the IoT space can create AI solutions that are not only efficient but also sustainable in the long run.

Overall, these case studies demonstrate the importance of optimizing AI models for real-time applications in various industries. By adopting techniques like Quantization, Compression, and Low-Rank Adaptation, professionals can make sophisticated AI capabilities more accessible, scalable, and cost-effective for a wider range of applications and businesses.

Chapter 8: Conclusion and Future Trends in AI Model Optimization

Summary of Techniques for Professionals

In the subchapter titled "Summary of Techniques for Professionals" in the book "Optimizing AI Models: Techniques for Professionals", we will discuss various techniques that professionals can utilize to optimize AI models. With the rising costs and scarcity of GPUs, there is a push towards optimizing AI models to be smaller and more efficient. Techniques like Low-Rank Adaptation (LoRA) and Quantization are helping make sophisticated AI capabilities accessible to smaller players and startups, reducing the dependency on large-scale infrastructure.

One technique discussed in this subchapter is Low-power AI models for edge computing. Edge computing allows AI models to be deployed closer to the data source, reducing latency and increasing efficiency. By optimizing AI models for low-power consumption, professionals can ensure that AI applications run smoothly on edge devices without draining too much power.

Another technique covered in this subchapter is Quantization techniques for reducing model size. Quantization involves reducing the precision of numerical values in the AI model, leading to a smaller model size without compromising performance. This technique is crucial for optimizing AI models for deployment on resource-constrained devices like mobile phones and IoT devices.

Compression algorithms for efficient model storage are also discussed in this subchapter. These algorithms help reduce the storage space required for AI models, making it easier to deploy and manage models on various devices. By utilizing compression algorithms, professionals can optimize AI models for efficient storage and deployment.

Lastly, this subchapter covers techniques for reducing inference latency in AI models. In real-time applications like autonomous vehicles and healthcare, reducing latency is crucial for ensuring timely and accurate results. Professionals can optimize AI models by implementing techniques that prioritize speed and efficiency, making them suitable for real-time applications. By incorporating these techniques into their workflow, professionals can ensure that their AI models are optimized for performance, accessibility, and efficiency in various applications.

Emerging Trends in AI Model Optimization

In the fast-paced world of artificial intelligence (AI), staying ahead of emerging trends in model optimization is crucial for professionals in the field. With the rising costs and scarcity of GPUs, there is a growing emphasis on making AI models smaller and more efficient. This push towards optimization is opening up opportunities for smaller players and startups to harness sophisticated AI capabilities. Techniques like Low-Rank Adaptation (LoRA) and Quantization are playing a key role in reducing the dependency on large-scale infrastructure, making AI more accessible to a wider range of users.

One of the key emerging trends in AI model optimization is the development of low-power models for edge computing. These models are designed to run efficiently on devices with limited computing power, such as smartphones and IoT devices. By optimizing AI models for edge computing, professionals can ensure that AI applications can run smoothly and efficiently in real-world settings.

Quantization techniques are also playing a significant role in the optimization of AI models. By reducing the precision of model weights and activations, quantization can dramatically reduce the size of AI models without sacrificing performance. This is particularly important for applications where model size is a limiting factor, such as mobile devices and IoT devices. By implementing quantization techniques, professionals can create more compact and resource-efficient AI models.

Another important trend in AI model optimization is the development of compression algorithms for efficient model storage. These algorithms allow professionals to reduce the size of AI models without compromising their performance, making it easier to store and deploy models in a variety of environments. By utilizing compression algorithms, professionals can optimize their AI models for a range of applications, from healthcare to autonomous vehicles.

Overall, staying informed about emerging trends in AI model optimization is essential for professionals working in the field. By leveraging techniques like low-power models, quantization, and compression algorithms, professionals can create more efficient and accessible AI models for a wide range of applications. With the right tools and strategies, professionals can stay ahead of the curve and continue to drive innovation in the field of AI model optimization.

Recommendations for Professionals in Model Optimization

In the ever-evolving landscape of AI technology, professionals in the field of model optimization must stay abreast of the latest techniques and strategies to ensure their models are efficient and accessible. With the rising costs and scarcity of GPUs, there is a growing need for smaller and more efficient AI models. To address this challenge, professionals should consider employing techniques such as Low-Rank Adaptation (LoRA) and Quantization. These methods can help make sophisticated AI capabilities accessible to smaller players and startups, reducing the dependency on large-scale infrastructure.

One key area of focus for professionals in model optimization should be developing low-power AI models for edge computing. By creating models that can run efficiently on edge devices, professionals can expand the reach of AI technology to a wider range of applications. Additionally, utilizing quantization techniques to reduce model size can further enhance the efficiency of AI models for edge computing, making them more accessible and cost-effective.

Another important recommendation for professionals in model optimization is to explore compression algorithms for efficient model storage. By implementing compression techniques, professionals can reduce the memory footprint of AI models without sacrificing performance. This is particularly important for mobile devices, IoT devices, and other resource-constrained environments where storage space is limited.

Furthermore, professionals should consider optimizing their AI models specifically for healthcare applications. Developing resource-efficient models that can run efficiently on healthcare devices can improve patient care and streamline medical processes. Similarly, optimizing AI models for autonomous vehicles can enhance safety and performance in the transportation industry.

In conclusion, professionals in model optimization must continuously explore new techniques and strategies to ensure their AI models are efficient, accessible, and scalable. By prioritizing techniques such as low-rank adaptation, quantization, compression, and optimization for specific industries, professionals can stay ahead of the curve and make a significant impact in the field of AI technology.

www.ingramcontent.com/pod-product-compliance
Lightning Source LLC
Chambersburg PA
CBHW082242220526
45479CB00005B/1314